California Sea Lion

by Jen Green

Consultants:

John E. McCosker, PhD
Chair of Aquatic Biology, California Academy of Sciences

Maureen Flannery, MS
Ornithology and Mammalogy Collection Manager, California Academy of Sciences

Wallace J. Nichols, PhD
Research Associate, California Academy of Sciences

BEARPORT PUBLISHING

New York, New York

Credits

Cover, © Imagebroker/FLPA; 3, © A. Cotton Photo/Shutterstock; 4, © Bruce Guenard/Biosphoto/FLPA; 5, © Doug Perrine/Seapics.com; 6, © Phillip Colla/Seapics.com; 7, © Wyland/Seapics.com; 8, © Phillip Colla/Seapics.com; 9, © Michael S. Nolan/Seapics.com; 10, © Franco Banfi/Getty Images; 11, © Phillip Colla/Seapics.com; 12, © Tobias Fridrich/Seapics.com; 13T, © Shutterstock; 13CL, © Rich Carey/Shutterstock; 13B, © Bruno Vittorio/Shutterstock; 13, © Norbert Wu/Minden Pictures/FLPA; 14T, © Frederic/Shutterstock; 14B, © Norbert Probst/Imagebroker/Photoshot; 15, © Eldad Yitzhak/Shutterstock; 16, © Franco Banfi/Getty Images; 17, © Suzi Eszterhas/Minden Pictures/FLPA; 18, © Suzi Eszterhas/Minden Pictures/FLPA; 19, © Phillip Colla/Seapics.com; 20, © Tui De Roy/Minden Pictures/Corbis; 21, © Norbert Wu/Minden Pictures/Corbis; 22BL, © Shutterstock; 22BR, © Natalie Jean/Shutterstock; 23TL, ©Photoshot; 23TC, © Image Quest Marine; 23TR, © Authur Morris/Corbis; 23BL, © Frans Lanting/Corbis; 23BC, © Phillip Colla/Seapics.com; 23BR, © Dean/Pennala/Shutterstock.

Publisher: Kenn Goin
Editorial Director: Adam Siegel
Creative Director: Spencer Brinker
Photo Researcher: Brown Bear Books Ltd

Library of Congress Cataloging-in-Publication Data

Green, Jen.
  California sea lion / by Jen Green.
     p. cm. — (The deep end: animal life underwater)
  Includes bibliographical references and index.
  ISBN-13: 978-1-61772-919-5 (library binding) — ISBN-10: 1-61772-919-1 (library binding)
  1. California sea lion—Juvenile literature. I. Title.
  QL737.P63G738 2014
  599.79'75—dc23
                              2013011505

For more information, write to Bearport Publishing Company, Inc., 45 West 21st Street, Suite 3B, New York, New York 10010. Printed in the United States of America.

10 9 8 7 6 5 4 3 2 1

Contents

An Ocean Home

A sea lion is swimming off the California coast.

Suddenly, it spots a group of fish in the deep water below.

The sea lion quickly dives down to catch one.

Soon, it returns to the water's surface with a fish between its sharp teeth.

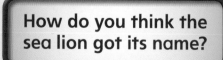

How do you think the sea lion got its name?

sea lion diving for food

On Land and at Sea

Sea lions are skillful swimmers, yet they are not fish.

They are **mammals** that live mainly in the sea.

They come on **shore** to rest, sit in the sun, and have babies.

The rest of the time they swim, float, and play in the ocean.

Sea lions got their name because males sometimes roar like lions.

Canada

Pacific Ocean

United States

Atlantic Ocean

Mexico

N
W E
S

Where California sea lions live

male California sea lion roaring

mother California
sea lion

Sea lions
are a kind of
seal. There are six
types of sea lions
found in oceans
around the
world.

young California
sea lions

Fast in the Water, Slower on Land

California sea lions swim faster than other kinds of sea lions and seals.

They can reach a top speed of 25 miles per hour (40 kph).

That's five times faster than the fastest human swimmer!

On land, they move more slowly.

They use their flippers like legs to walk and even run.

flipper

California sea lions are among the fastest animals in the ocean. At top speeds, they often leap above the water as they race along.

leaping sea lions

What do you think makes a California sea lion such a fast swimmer?

Built for Speed

A California sea lion has a long, sleek body and powerful flippers.

Its shape allows it to move easily through water, like a submarine.

Its front flippers help the animal quickly pull itself forward.

Its back flippers help it control the direction in which it is swimming.

How do you think being a fast swimmer helps a sea lion?

back flipper

sleek body

Male California sea lions grow to a length of about eight feet (2.4 m). Females grow to be about six feet (1.8 m) long.

front flipper

Finding a Meal

Being fast swimmers helps sea lions catch **prey**.

They chase many kinds of fish, squid, and octopuses.

To find these animals, they use their excellent eyesight and hearing.

In deep water that has little light, sea lions use their whiskers to help them find prey.

A sea lion's whiskers can feel the ripples made by other swimming animals.

whiskers

fish

squid

octopus

When swimming underwater, a sea lion can hold its breath for up to ten minutes.

California sea lion

Which animals in the ocean might hunt sea lions?

Keeping Safe

While California sea lions hunt for food, other animals hunt them.

Killer whales chase sea lions at high speeds.

Great white sharks sneak up on and attack sea lions, especially the young or sick.

Sea lions swim as fast as they can to escape from their enemies.

If they are near shore, they will run onto land for safety.

killer whale

great white shark

Sharks usually attack sea lions when they are floating and resting on the water's surface.

Besides escaping from an enemy, why else might a sea lion leave the water?

Out of the Water

Sea lions leave the water when it's time to start a family.

In spring and summer, adult male and female sea lions come onto land to **mate**.

The following spring or summer the female gives birth to one **pup**.

Like all mammal babies, the pup drinks its mother's milk.

pup

mother

A sea lion pup can walk about 30 minutes after it is born. A few weeks later, the pup's mother teaches her pup how to swim.

mother

pup

17

Group Living

Female sea lions often raise their pups with other mothers and pups.

They all live together in a **rookery**, which has hundreds of pups.

At times, the mothers must return to the ocean to hunt for food.

While some mothers are hunting, others will stay with the pups at the rookery.

When the mothers return from hunting, each one finds her baby by listening for its call.

mother and pup

A mother sea lion recognizes her baby's smell as well as its call. The baby also recognizes its mother in the same way.

sea lion rookery

Growing Up

After six months, sea lion pups can hunt in the ocean for their own food.

They also enjoy playing with the adults.

They spin, twirl, and do somersaults in the water.

After about three years, pups leave their mothers to live on their own.

When they go, the pups are ready for a long life in their ocean home!

pups playing

A California sea lion may live up to 15 years.

Science Lab

Be a Sea Lion Scientist

Imagine you are a scientist who studies California sea lions. Write a diary about the animals' activities.

Describe what sea lions do in the water and what they do on land. Draw pictures to include in your diary.

Use the information in this book to help you.

When you are finished, share your diary and drawings with friends and family.

Here are some words that you can use to write about a California sea lion's home.

ocean   enemies   swim

shore   hunt   pups

Read the questions below and think about the answers.

You can include some of the information from your answers in your diary.

- *Where do California sea lions spend their time?*

- *Why are sea lions able to swim so fast?*

- *What foods do California sea lions like to eat?*

- *What dangers do sea lions face in the ocean?*

Science Words

mammals (MAM-uhlz) warm-blooded animals that drink their mothers' milk as babies

mate (MAYT) to come together in order to have young

prey (PRAY) an animal that is hunted by another animal for food

pup (PUP) a baby sea lion

rookery (RUK-er-ee) a place where young sea lions grow up together

shore (SHOR) the land along the edge of an ocean, river, or lake

Index

Read More

Johnson, Jinny. *Sea Lion.* North Mankato, MN: Smart Apple Media (2007).

Lunis, Natalie. *California Sea Lion: Fast and Smart! (Blink of an Eye: Superfast Animals!).* New York: Bearport (2011).

Sexton, Colleen A. *Sea Lions (Oceans Alive).* Minneapolis, MN: Bellwether Media (2008).

Learn More Online

To learn more about California sea lions, visit **www.bearportpublishing.com/TheDeepEnd**

About the Author

Jen Green has been interested in natural history since she was a child. She has written dozens of children's books on subjects as varied as raccoons, gophers, and termites. She loves walking in her native Sussex, England.